A Message of Peace

by

Ḥaḍrat Mirzā Ghulām Aḥmad[as]
The Promised Messiah and Mahdī
Founder of the Aḥmadiyyah Muslim Jamāʿat

A Message Of Peace
(Originally published in Urdu as *Paighām-e-Ṣulḥ*)

An English rendering of "Paighām-e-Ṣulḥ", the last written work of Ḥaḍrat Mirzā Ghulām Aḥmad[as], The Promised Messiah & Mahdī— Founder of the Aḥmadiyyah Muslim Jamāʿat.

Translated into English by: Team of Lajna Imāʾillah, UK
Revised by: Munawar A. Saeed and Fouzan M. Pal

First edition published in Pakistan in 1968 [*Message of Peace*].
Second edition (completely new translation) published in UK in 1996
 [*A Message of Peace*, ISBN: 1 85372 566 8].
Third edition (revised translation) published in UK in 2007
Reprinted in UK in 2015

© **Islam International Publications Ltd.**

Published by:
 Islam International Publications Ltd.
 "Islamabad"
 Sheephatch Lane
 Tilford, Surrey GU10 2AQ
 United Kingdom

Printed in the UK at:
 Raqeem Press
 Tilford, Surrey, GU10 2AQ

For more information, please visit www.alislam.org

ISBN 1 85372 958 2
10 9 8 7 6 5 4 3 2

PUBLISHER'S NOTE

Paighām-e-Ṣulḥ (A Message of Peace) is the last written work of Ḥaḍrat Mirzā Ghulām Aḥmad, the Promised Messiah[as], the Founder of the Aḥmadiyyah Muslim Jamā'at. It was completed on May 25, 1908—just a day before his demise. The citizens of Lahore were the primary audience for this address; however its subject matter is in no way confined to them alone but is of vital importance to the entire population of the Indian subcontinent. The general principles laid down in the work are applicable to all countries which host multiple religions.

The Promised Messiah[as] passed away on May 26, 1908. The address was read out on his behalf at a conference held on June 21, 1908 at the Punjab University, Lahore for which it was intended. The English rendering of the address was done by a board of translators under the supervision and auspices of Ḥaḍrat Mirzā Ṭāhir Aḥmad[rta], the Fourth Head of the worldwide Aḥmadiyyah Muslim Jamā'at. The board consisted of: Sheila Aḥmad Malik, Farīna Qureshī, Ṣofia Ṣafī, Farzānā Jāved, Farhānā Ṣādiq, Fauzia Bājwa, Nawīda Shāhid and Fauzia Shāh. The present revision done by Munawar Aḥmed Saeed and Fouzan Pāl is published with the approval of Ḥaḍrat

Mirzā Masroor Aḥmad[aba], the present Head of the Aḥmadiyyah Muslim Jamā'at. Other members of the USA translation team who made valuable contributions to this revision include Aḥmad Ṭāriq and 'Abdul Wahab Mirzā. May Allah bestow them the best reward for this. *Āmīn.*

This book uses the following system of transliteration adopted by the Royal Asiatic Society.

- ا at the beginning of a word, pronounced as *a, i, u* preceded by a very slight aspiration, like *h* in the English word *honour*.

- ث *th*, pronounced like *th* in the English word *thing*.

- ح *ḥ*, a guttural aspirate, stronger than *h*.

- خ *kh*, pronounced like the Scotch *ch* in *loch*.

- ذ *dh*, pronounced like the English *th* in *that*.

- ص *ṣ*, strongly articulated *s*.

- ض *ḍ*, similar to the English *th* in *this*.

- ط *ṭ*, strongly articulated palatal *t*.

- ظ *ẓ*, strongly articulated *z*.

- ع *'*, a strong guttural sound, the pronunciation of which must be learnt by the ear.

- غ *gh*, a sound approached very nearly by *r* in the French *grasseye* and also the German *r*. It requires the muscles of the throat to be in the gargling position whilst pronouncing it.

ق   *q*, a deep guttural *k* sound.

ء   ', a sort of catch in the voice.

Short vowels are represented by '*a*' for ◌َ (like '*u*' in '*bud*'); '*i*' for ◌ِ (like '*i*' in '*bid*'); '*u*' for ◌ُ (like '*oo*' in '*wood*'); the long vowels by '*ā*' for ◌ٰ or آ (like '*a*' in '*father*'); '*ī*' for ی ◌ؔ or ◌ٖ (like '*ee*' in '*deep*'); '*ai*' for ی ◌َ (like '*i*' in '*site*'); '*ū*' for و ◌ُ (like '*oo*' in '*root*'): '*au*' for, و ◌َ (resembling '*ou*' in '*sound*').

Please note that in transliterated words the letter '*e*' is to be pronounced as in '*prey*' which rhymes with '*day*'; however the pronunciation is flat without the element of English diphthong. If in Urdu and Persian words, letter '*e*' is lengthened a bit more it is transliterated as '*ei*', to be pronounced as '*ei*' in '*feign*' without the element of diphthong; thus کے is transliterated as '*Kei*'.

The consonants not included in the above list have the same phonetic value as in the principal languages of Europe.

The following abbreviations have been used. Readers are urged to recite the full salutations:

sa   *ṣal-lallāhu 'alaihi wa sallam*, meaning 'may the peace and blessings of Allah be upon him' is written after the name of the Holy Prophet Muḥammad[sa].

as   *'alaihis salām*, meaning 'peace be upon him' is written after the names of Prophets other than the Holy Prophet Muḥammad[sa].

ra	*raḍi-Allāhu 'anhu/'anhā/'anhum*, meaning 'may Allah be pleased with him/her/them' is written after the names of the Companions of the Holy Prophet Muhammad[sa] or of the Promised Messiah[as].
rta	*raḥmatullāh 'alaih*, meaning 'may Allah shower His mercy upon him' is written after the names of deceased pious Muslims who are not Companions of the Holy Prophet Muhammad[sa] or of the Promised Messiah[as].
aba	*ayyadahullāhu ta'ālā bi naṣrihil 'azīz*, meaning 'may Allah support him with His Mighty Help' is written after the name of the current *Khalīfah* of the Promised Messiah[as].

Please note that in referencing the Holy Qur'an, we have counted 'In the name of Allah, the Gracious, the Merciful' as the first verse of the Chapter in which it appears.

We pray to God that this message may reach all people who have a genuine desire to study these issues. May Allah make this a source of guidance for them. *Āmīn*.

Munir-ud-Din Shams
Additional Vakīl-ut-Taṣnīf
March 2007

ABOUT THE AUTHOR

The worldwide Aḥmadiyyah Muslim Jamāʿat was founded in 1889. Its founder, Ḥaḍrat Mirzā Ghulām Aḥmad[as] of Qadian, India, claimed to be the Promised Messiah and Reformer whose advent was awaited under different names and titles by the adherents of various religions. Under Divine guidance, Ḥaḍrat Mirzā Ghulām Aḥmad[as] revealed that only one such reformer was to appear and that his mission was to bring mankind into the fold of a single universal religion, Islam. He also maintained that the Promised Reformer was to appear as a subordinate and follower of the Holy Prophet of Islam, Muḥammad [may peace and blessings of Allah be upon him]—in accordance with the prophecies by him about the second coming of Messiah and the appearance of *al-Imām, al-Mahdī* from among the Muslims. He claimed to be the person in whom these prophecies were fulfilled.

Image of
Title Page of the First Edition
(Written & Printed in 1908)

A Message of Peace

written by
Ḥaḍrat Mirzā Ghulām Aḥmad
The Promised Messiah (peace be upon him)

$$\text{بِسْمِ اللّٰهِ الرَّحْمٰنِ الرَّحِيْمِ}^1$$
$$\text{نَحْمَدُهٗ وَنُصَلِّىْ عَلٰى رَسُوْلِهِ الْكَرِيْمِ}^2$$

O my Almighty God, my Beloved Guide! Show us the path which leads the righteous and the sincere to Thee. And save us from treading the path which leads to carnal desires, malice, spite and worldly pursuits.

Having done that, I now draw your attention to the following: notwithstanding the hundreds of differences between us, Muslims and Hindus alike share one thing in common, i.e., we all believe in God, the Creator and Master of the Universe. Also, we belong to the same denomination of God's species and are referred to as humans. Furthermore, as inhabitants of the same country, we are mutual neighbours. This requires that we become friends to each other, with purity of heart and sincerity of intentions. We should dispose kindly to each other and be mutually helpful. In the

---

1. In the name of Allah, the Gracious, the Merciful. [Publisher]
2. We praise Him and send blessings on His exalted Prophet[sa]. [Publisher]

difficulties pertaining to religious and worldly matters, we should exercise such sympathy towards each other as if we have become limbs of the same body.

My countrymen, a religion which does not inculcate universal compassion is no religion at all. Similarly, a human being without the faculty of compassion is no human at all. Our God has never discriminated between one people and another. This is illustrated by the fact that all the potentials and capabilities which have been granted to the Āryans have also been granted to the races inhabiting Arabia, Persia, Syria, China, Japan, Europe and America. The earth created by God provides a common floor for all people alike, and His sun and moon and many stars are a source of radiance and provide many other benefits to all alike. Likewise, all peoples benefit from the elements created by Him, such as air, water, fire and earth, and similarly from other products created by Him like grain, fruit, and healing agents, etc. These attributes of God teach us the lesson that we, too, should behave magnanimously and kindly towards our fellow human beings and should not be petty of heart and illiberal.

Friends! Take it as certain that if either of our two nations would not treat God's attributes with respect and will not shape its conduct in accordance with the conduct of God, then, that nation will soon be wiped out from the face of the earth. Not only will it destroy itself but it will also jeopardise the future of its generations to come. The righteous of all ages have testified that following God's ways works like an elixir for the people. Moreover the survival, both physical and spiritual, of human beings depends on the same eternal truth that man should follow the virtuous attributes of God Who is the Fountainhead of all that is essential for survival.

God commences the Holy Qur'an with the following verse which is contained in *sūrah al-Fātiḥah*:[3]

اَلْحَمْدُ لِلّٰهِ رَبِّ الْعٰلَمِيْنَ ۞

That is, all perfect and holy attributes belong exclusively to Allah, Who is the Lord of all the worlds.

The word *'ālam* comprises all different peoples, all different ages and all the different countries. The commencement of the Holy Qur'an with this verse was designed to counter the views of such people as attempted to monopolise God's unlimited providence for their own nation and imagined that the other nations did not belong to God or that having created these other people, God discarded them as being of no consequence, or else perhaps they were shelved to oblivion by Him, or (God forbid) they were not even created by Him.

To illustrate this further, we refer to the view of the Jews and the Christians, still commonly held by them, that all the Prophets and Messengers of God belonged only to the House of Israel, and that God completely ignored the religious and spiritual requirements of other people, as though He were displeased with them and that, despite finding them in manifest error and ignorance, He showed least concern for their spiritual welfare. As is also written in the Gospels that Jesus Christ (peace be on him) observed that he had been sent only for the lost sheep of Israel.[4]

---

3. (*al-Fātiḥah*, 1:2) [Publisher]
4. But he answered and said, I am not sent but unto the lost sheep of the house of Israel. (*Matthew*, 15:24) [Publisher]

Impossible as it is, yet by way of argument let us assume that Jesus[as] did claim to be God. In that case, for him to confine his beneficence to such a small circle as the House of Israel does not behove the magnanimity of God. Had he been God, was he God only for the House of Israel to the exclusion of all other nations? He is known to have suggested that he had no concern for those who did not belong to the House of Israel.

In short, the Jews and the Christians do believe that all Prophets and Messengers have been appearing from among them, and that Divine scriptures were revealed to them alone. Thereafter, according to the beliefs of the Christians, the institution of revelation and communion with God ended with Jesus Christ (peace be upon him) as though a seal had been set on the institution of revelation from God.

Unfortunately the Hindus of the Āryā sect also entertain a similar belief. Like the Jews and Christians, who restrict the institution of Prophethood and Divine revelation exclusively to their people and deny the honour of Divine revelation to others, the Āryās also, unfortunately for the human race, have adopted the same doctrine. They too believe that the blessing of Divine communication was never bestowed to any people outside the domain of the Āryan race. Again it is India alone which, according to them, is exclusively blessed by God for the selection of the four 'Rishīs' from its soil; it is Sanskrit alone, the language of the Vedas, which has always been the medium of instruction chosen by God. One can safely conclude from this, that both these nations do not consider God to be the Lord [Provident] of all the worlds. Notwithstanding this, He is still proclaimed to be Lord of the Universe and not that of the Israelites or the Āryans alone. Moreover this strange behaviour of God, as presented by them, draws an image of God which is so partial that He appears unmindful of the rest of His creation. Thus, it is for the refutation of such erroneous views, that God commences the Holy Qur'an with the verse:[5]

$$ٱلْحَمْدُ لِلَّهِ رَبِّ الْعَٰلَمِيْنَ ۝$$

God also made it clear in several places in the Holy Qur'an that His Messengers have been appearing in different lands all over the world. In fact He did not neglect any people or any country. The Holy Qur'an explains through various examples that just as God has been looking after the physical development of the people of every country, in accordance with their requirements, so has He blessed every country and every people with spiritual upbringing. Allah says in the Holy Qur'an:[6]

$$... وَاِنْ مِّنْ اُمَّةٍ اِلَّا خَلَا فِيْهَا نَذِيْرٌ ۝$$

Meaning that there is no people to whom a Warner has not been sent.

Therefore there is no question that the True and Perfect God, to believe in Whom is essential for every person, is the Lord of all the worlds. Furthermore, His providence is not confined to any particular people, age or country. In fact, He is the Lord of all peoples, the Lord of time and space, and He is the Sovereign of all the countries. He alone is the

---

5. All praise belongs to Allah, Lord of all the worlds.
   (al-Fātiḥah, 1:2) [Publisher]
6. (Fāṭir, 35:25)

Fountainhead of all beneficence and the Source of every physical and spiritual strength. All that exists is sustained by Him. He is the Support for every creature.

It is the universal beneficence of God which encompasses all peoples, all countries and all ages. It so happened lest anyone should have cause to complain that: 'God has bestowed His favour upon such and such people, but not upon us.' Or that: 'So and so received the Book in order to be guided while we did not.' Or that: 'In such and such an age, He revealed Himself through His revelations, communications and miracles but in our time He remained hidden.' Thus, by demonstrating His universal beneficence, He left no justification for such possible accusations. He displayed His virtues boundlessly so that no people remain bereft of physical and spiritual bounties from Him. He also did not treat any age as doomed.

So, when such are the attributes of our Lord, it is but befitting for us to acquire them ourselves. So, O compatriots! This short epistle entitled *A Message of Peace* is being presented to you with all due respects and with a sincere heartfelt prayer that Almighty God may Himself inspire you and fill your hearts with trust in my sincerity, lest you misread this friendly gesture and consider it to be an attempt to gain some ulterior motive. Dear Countrymen! The matter of the Hereafter is very often obscured to ordinary people. Its secrets are known only to a few of the enlightened, who embrace a kind of death [for the sake of their Lord] before they actually die. The goodness of this world, on the other hand, is easily recognised by any man with vision and wisdom.

It is a common experience that calamities which cannot be averted by ordinary measures, and the difficulties which seem insurmountable, very often respond to the power of unanimity. Hence it would be against the dictates of wisdom for one to not benefit from the blessings of unanimity. The Hindus and the Muslims are two great nations inhabiting this country. It is hard to believe that either of the two, for instance the Hindus, would one day gain total domination over the Muslims, and turn them out of this country altogether. Likewise, it is not possible for Muslims to expel the Hindus from their homeland. It should always be borne in mind that Hindus and Muslims are indispensable to each other in this country. If one is beset with a calamity, the other will inescapably share it. If either one intends to humiliate the other, out of egoistic pride or vanity, then it will not escape the consequent disgrace itself. And if anyone among them falls short of showing concern for his neighbour, then he too will suffer the ill effect of his callousness. Anyone who contemplates annihilation of the other is like one who saws off the branch on which he is sitting. With the Grace of Allah, you have also got a measure of education; it behoves you now to eschew grudge and promote mutual love. Similarly, the dictates of your wisdom require that you abandon the course of callousness and adopt an attitude of compassion and sympathy. The hardship of this life is like unto a journey in a desert in the midst of summer on a hot sunny day. It would be futile to take this arduous journey without cool water. It is the cool water of mutual love which you so direly need to extinguish this burning fire and to save you from dying of thirst.

In precarious times such as these I invite you to truce, as reconciliation is urgently required by both nations. Many a calamity is befalling the world; there are earthquakes and there are famines. Over and above the earthquakes and famines we continue to be plagued by the bubonic pestilence. Moreover the Divine revelations which God has conveyed to me further confirm that if people do not mend their evil ways and practices and do not repent their sins, the world will be further visited by other severe calamities. One misery will not end before another follows. Eventually people will reach the end of their tether and will wonder what is happening to them and what next is in store for them. They will be pushed to the edge of their senses by calamity upon calamity. So take heed my countrymen, before such evil days confront you. It is highly essential that Hindus and the Muslims should come to terms with each other and if either of the two parties is guilty of such excesses as obstruct the path of peace, they are better advised to desist from pursuing that course. Otherwise, the entire blame for the sin of mutual enmity will be borne by the faulting party.

If someone questions the possibility of reaching reconciliation while religious differences are playing such a negative role, throwing hearts further apart, then my answer would be to say that difference in matters of religion can only play a negative role when it disregards the dictates of justice, wisdom and the well-tested human values. It is to avoid this danger that man has been fully fortified with a clear sense of judgement and common sense. He should thus always carve a path for himself which never deviates from the path of justice and good sense. Again it should not violate the commonly experienced human sensibilities. Also it should be remembered that day to day petty differences cannot obstruct the course of reconciliation. Only those differences can destroy the process of reconciliation which result in insulting and blasphemous attitudes by one towards the revered Messengers and revealed holy books of the other.

The good news in all this for those who seek reconciliation is that all of the Islamic teachings are also found in the different parts of Vedic teaching. For instance, although the newborn branch of Vedic faith entitled Āryā Samāj teaches that after the revelation of the Vedas, communication from God to man was sealed, the great avatārs born in the Hindu faith from time to time, who have millions upon millions of followers in this country, have doubtlessly broken that seal by claiming to be recipients of Divine revelation. One such elect Divine representative, who is greatly revered in this country and Bengal, is known as Srī Krishnā. He claimed to be the recipient of God's Word and his followers not only believe him to be a Messenger but some consider him to be God personified. There is no doubt, however, that Srī Krishnā was a Messenger and a representative of God in his time, and God conversed with him.

Likewise, from among the Hindu people of the Latter Days was one named Bābā Nānak, whose saintliness has become a byword in this country. His followers, the Sikhs, number no less than two million. Bābā Ṣāḥib openly claims to be the recipient of revelation in the Janam Sākhīs[7] and the Granth[8]. In one Janam Sākhī he states that he had received

---

7. Autobiographies of Bābā Nānak. [Publisher]
8. The Holy Book of the Sikhs. [Publisher]

revelation from God testifying to the truth of Islam. Based on this he performed Ḥajj[9] and followed the Islamic injunctions meticulously. It is established without doubt that great signs and miracles were manifested by him. It goes without question that Bābā Nānak was a holy and pious man. He was one of those whom God, the Mighty, the Glorious, made drink out of His goblet of love. He was born among Hindus only to bear witness that Islam is from God. Anyone who sees for himself his relics preserved at Derā Nānak, in which he has testified to the *kalimah*[10]:

$$\text{لَآ اِلٰهَ اِلَّا اللّٰهُ مُحَمَّدٌ رَّسُوْلُ اللّٰهِ}$$

and witnesses relics that lie enshrined at Gūrū Hersahaī, District Ferozepur, among which is also a copy of the Holy Qur'an[11], how can he ever doubt the fact that because of his pure heart, nature and effort, Bābā Nānak had come to know of the secret that lay hidden from the so-called Pundits. Gūrū Bābā Nānak also claimed to be a recipient of revelation from God and he enjoyed the Divine blessing of showing many miracles. Thus he roundly debunked the erroneous claims that there was no revelation after the Vedas or that no signs were manifested thereafter. No doubt Bābā Nānak was a great blessing from God for the adherents of Hinduism. You may

---

9. The pilgrimage to Ka'bah, the house of Allah in Mecca, Saudi Arabia. [Publisher]
10. There is none worthy of worship except Allah; Muḥammad is the messenger of Allah. [Publisher]
11. Bābā Nānak carried a copy of the Holy Qur'an in a small bag throughout his journeys. This small sized copy is termed *Hamayal* which means 'pendant' because many Godly people carried it suspended from their shoulders. [Publisher]

deem him, if you please, the last avatar for Hinduism who endeavoured to eradicate the hatred which Hindus had for Islam. But it is tragic for this country that Hindu faith did not derive any benefit from this Divine blessing which came in the person of Bābā Nānak. On the contrary, the Pundits inflicted much pain upon him for praising Islam wherever he went. It was his mission in fact to bring Hinduism and Islam to a state of mutual peace. Unfortunately for this country, the followers of the Hindu faith paid no due attention to his teaching. If he and his pious teachings had been shown any respect, the Hindus and the Muslims would have become united by now. O grief that such a righteous man came into this world, remained with us and passed away, but the imprudent did not gain any benefit from his light!

In any case, he proved that the institution of revelation and communion never terminates and that the Divine signs of Allah always appear through the agency of His chosen ones and he stood witness to the fact that harbouring enmity towards Islam is tantamount to harbouring enmity towards the Divine light.

Similarly, I can also, from personal experience, give testimony that the present age has certainly not been deprived of communication and revelation from God. On the contrary, God still speaks as He used to speak and still hears as He used to hear. It is not that His eternal attributes have become inoperative. I have been blessed with communication from God for nearly thirty years, and He has shown at my hand hundreds of signs which have been observed by thousands of witnesses and have also been widely published in books and newspapers. Without exception, people from all denominations have witnessed one or another of the signs.

In the face of such repeated evidence, the teaching of the Āryā Samāj, which is wrongfully attributed to Vedas, cannot be accepted, for it alleges that all Divine revelation and communication has come to an end with the Vedas. This Āryā position is tantamount to believing that nothing is left of man's belief but tales and legends. Consequent upon this dogma, they dismiss all the Divine scriptures that came after the Vedas as mere man-made fabrications. They do this notwithstanding the fact that the Divine scriptures in question possess a greater and more potent proof of the Divine origin than the Vedas. The hand of God's support and assistance is behind them and extraordinary signs from God bear witness to their truth. By what logic, then, are the Vedas termed the 'Word of God', while these other books are not? The attributes of God are limitlessly profound and He lies hidden behind innumerable covers. Hence, dictates of wisdom require that He should not rely on one book alone for His manifestation. Rather, it is befitting for Him to choose His Messengers from all over the world in different countries, reflecting His glory through them by blessing them with His revelation and gift of communion. This is so that man, weak and credulous by nature, should not be deprived of the good fortune of responding to His call.

Pure common sense cannot accept the proposition that God, the Lord of the Universe, Who illuminates the East and West alike with His radiant sun and quenches the thirst of every land with the universal bounty of His rain, should be so miserly (God forbid!) with regards to the spiritual needs of man as to become partial only to one country, one people and one language. I fail to understand what logic and rationale it is that God the Omniscient listens to man's prayers and supplications and understands him in every language, and He is not displeased with it, yet He abhors to make His word descend upon hearts in any language other than Sanskrit, the language of the Vedas. This philosophy is found only in the Vedas like a well concealed enigma which no one, as yet, has been able to resolve.

Personally, I consider the Vedas to be absolved of ever having displayed such a philosophy upon any of its pages, which not only goes against common sense, but also blemishes God with the allegation of miserliness and niggardly conduct. The reality is that once a long time elapses after the revelation of a Divine Book, the followers of that Book, either out of sheer ignorance, or as a result of some ulterior motives—by mistake or by intent—feel free to annotate the Divine teachings. Because these annotators are of divergent views, so, with the passage of time, hundreds of denominations are born out of one.

It is also strange that just as the Āryās believe that revelation has only been confined to the Āryā kith and kin and Āryā faith, and that Sanskrit has been specifically employed by God as His own language, so too the Jews have similar views regarding the chosen Children of Israel and their Books. They believe that the only language of God is Hebrew and the institution of revelation has been confined to the House of Israel and its land. According to them, anyone who claims to be a prophet of God while he does not belong to this House and does not speak their language is (God forbid) definitely a liar.

Is it not then a strange coincidence, that both these peoples have followed the same path in their dogmatic assertions? Likewise, the followers of many other religions entertain similar views, as for example, the Zoroastrians, who claim that their religion originated billions of years before the Vedic revelation. From this it transpires that the tendency (to confine the revelation of God to one's own language or the Book) is based merely on prejudice and ignorance. This is further abetted by the fact that in the dark ages of the past, people had no access to the information concerning people and countries beyond the boundaries of their homelands. This lack of knowledge on their part led them to draw the wrong conclusions. They had witnessed that God had bestowed upon them a Divine teaching in the form of a Book, and they knew that Messengers of God had been selected from among themselves; hence their erroneous impression that they had been the only people so favourably treated by God, while the rest of the world was unfortunate in being deprived of this blessing.

This erroneous view has done a lot of damage to the world, and it has worked as a seed of mutual enmity and malice which continues to grow. For a long time, it so happened that a people remained hidden from others and one country remained concealed and veiled from the other to the extent that the scholars of the Āryā faith used to believe that there was no inhabitation beyond the Himalayas.

When God lifted the veil, it was already too late for them to mend. By this time they were already fixed in their prejudices. All the false distinctive features which people had attributed to their own revealed books, divines, and messengers, had become deeply rooted in their hearts and had become permanently fixed like the etching on stones. Each people had the same misconception that God's capital was situated in their country. Savage behaviour was predominant among most people of that age. Hence, to them the sword seemed a natural instrument for settling accounts with those people who dared to oppose the old order. Who then would dare to cool down their self-aggrandisement to create an atmosphere conducive to mutual peace?

Gautum Buddha was one brave enough who stood up to achieve this goal. He did not agree with the erroneous view that the Vedas are everything and that there is nothing beyond them. Nor did he believe in any people, country or tribe as being exceptional. In other words, he did not agree that the Vedas enjoyed a monopoly and it was only this faith, this language, this country, and the Brahmans which had been permanently and exclusively registered in the court records of God to become the recipients of His revelation. He suffered greatly because of expressing these different views and he was accused of being an atheist or an agnostic. Similarly scholars and researchers of Europe and America, who do not accept the godhead of Jesus[as], and whose hearts refuse to believe that God can be crucified, are atheists according to the Christian priests.

This is how Buddha was branded an atheist. As is the routine of the mischievous antagonists who incite the hatred of common people, he was made a target of many a false accusation. Consequently, he was turned out of the soil on which he was born and bred, the country that was his homeland. Even now, the Hindus view Buddhism with disdain and they begrudge its success. According to Jesus Christ (peace be on him) '**A Prophet is not without honour save in his own country.**'[12] Buddha migrated to another country and gained tremendous success there. It is reported that one third of the world is populated by the followers of Buddha. As far as the large majority of adherents is concerned, the real centre lies in China and Japan, but his message has reached as far as Southern Russia and America.

Now we return to the original subject of discussion: the age when one religion was unaware of the existence of the other. In that general state of ignorance, it was but natural that every people should have considered their own religion and their own book to be the only one. Eventually when countries became linked to each other through the spread of knowledge, this trend of monopolising God resulted in the creation of another obstacle in the path of mutual understanding. People began to expect the religions in every other country to agree with theirs, or else they stood rejected. It was no easy task to rid such religions of the poetical exaggerations built around them over the ages. So the followers of every religion braced themselves to vehemently oppose the other. So, also, the religion of Zend-Avesta raised the flag with the claim that, 'No one else is like us' and they monopolised the institution of prophethood to their own family. They related such a long history of their religion, that those who used to pride the longevity of Vedic history were put to shame.

---

12. See (*Mathew*, 13:57) and (*Mark*, 6:4). [Publisher]

In their turn, the faith of the Hebrews crossed every limit when they asserted that Syria was declared to be the eternal seat of God's sovereignty and that only the pious among them would be considered worthy of being sent for the reformation of the world. But in effect, the work of reformation remained limited to the House of Israel, and the revelation of God became the prerogative of only their House under the seal of God. All others who rose with a claim were considered liars and imposters.

Likewise, among the Āryās, similar views to those which were widespread among the Israelites gained favour. According to their belief, God is the King of the Āryās alone; a king of the type who is totally unaware of the existence of others. And without rhyme or reason, it is believed that God had forever set His heart on the Āryā climate. Little does He care to visit other countries once in a while, to inquire about the state of the miserable people living there whom He had once created only to forget them forever.

Dear friends! I appeal to you, in the name of God, to consider whether such views can really be entertained by human nature. Or if any conscience could find room for them within its bounds! I fail to understand what kind of logic it is that on the one hand God is conceived to be the Lord of the whole universe and, on the other, He is claimed to have withdrawn His hand of providence from a large part of the world, and that His gaze remains fixed on a particular people and one section of a particular country. O those who possess wisdom! Please decide with justice if, in the entire realm of physical laws created by God, there is a single piece of evidence in favour of this. Why then should His spiritual laws be based on such biased attitudes?

If the faculty of reasoning is employed, the good or evil of anything becomes manifest from the fruit it bears. Needless for me to discuss the consequences of abusing and reviling the holy Prophets of God, who have been seen and accepted by hundreds and millions of people; there is hardly a people who have not themselves witnessed the outcome of the bitter fruit of such practices.

O Dear Ones! Age-old experience and repeated trials have established, without question, that to insult and abuse the Prophets and Messengers of different countries and peoples is such a deadly poison which not only destroys the body but also kills the soul, thereby ruining the worldly prospects as well as the spiritual. A country whose inhabitants are always after finding faults in the leaders of others, and constantly assassinate their characters, can never rest in peace themselves. Such people can never achieve true unity who, individually or mutually, refer to each other's Prophets or saints or divines with malice or foul language. Who would not be outraged at the insults hurled at their Prophet or leader? In particular, Muslims are such people who, although they do not believe their Prophet to be God or the son of God, do regard him[sa] to be the most revered of all the holy men born of a human mother. To make peace with a sincere Muslim is not possible unless during discussion, their Holy Prophet[sa] is mentioned with respect and refined language.

As for us[13], we never use indecent language with regard to the Prophets of other peoples. In fact, we believe that for all the Prophets who have come to different peoples of the world

---

13. The Muslims [Publisher]

and have been accepted by millions of people in all parts of the world, and love for them and their greatness has been firmly established in any one part of the world, and further that this state of devotion and love for them has endured the test of time, is evidence enough of their truthfulness. Had they not been from God, they could not have been accepted on such a wide scale by millions upon millions of hearts. God does not bestow such honour upon those whom He favours not. If an imposter aspires to occupy their position, he is soon brought to ruin.

By virtue of the same logic, we believe the Vedas to be divine in origin and we consider their saints to be venerable and holy. We do so despite our observation that Vedic teaching has not succeeded, nor could it ever succeed, in turning any section of its followers into true worshippers of God. The people in this country who worship idols, fire, the sun, the Ganges, or thousands of deities, or who are adherents of Jainism or the Shakat faith, all claim their religion to originate from the Vedas. The Vedas are so vague that they permit all sects to deduce from them whatsoever they wish. However, in accordance with what we are taught by God, we believe that the original Vedas were not man's fabrication. A human fabrication lacks the power to establish a lasting order. Although we do not find any mention of stone worship in the Vedas, without a doubt, Vedic teaching is full of the mention of the worship of fire, air, water, the moon, the sun, and so on. There is no verse which prohibits the worship of these objects. Who is to say that the older sects of Hindus are false and only the new sect of Āryās is the true one? People who, by referring to the Vedas, worship these objects, are armed with the powerful argument that there is clear mention of such worship and nowhere is there any prohibition. To say that these are the names of God, is a claim which has not as yet been clearly settled. Had it been settled, what reason could there have been for the scholarly pundits in Banares and other cities to have rejected the beliefs of the Āryās? Despite efforts over the past thirty to thirty-five years, very few Hindus have accepted the Āryā faith and in comparison with the Sanatan faith and other Hindu sects, the followers of the Āryā faith number so few that they are insignificant, nor do they have any influence on the remaining Hindu sects. Similarly, the teachings of *nyog*, which is attributed to the Vedas, is abhorrent to human dignity and the human sense of honour. As I have already stated, we cannot accept that it is a genuine Vedic teaching. In fact, our well-meaning intentions make us strongly inclined to believe that such teachings must have been introduced later from sensual motives. Since thousands of years have passed since the original compilation of Vedas it is possible that in different times some scribes added to or subtracted from it. For us it is proof enough that the Āryā faith has had millions upon millions of followers for thousands of years who have held it to be the word of God. It is not possible that the work of an imposter could enjoy such honour.

So when we, despite all these obstacles, purely out of fear of God, accept the Vedas to be divine revelation in its origin and assume all the false teachings to be the work of scribes, what justification can there be for the Holy Qur'an to be made the target of such brutal attacks? It is full of injunctions from cover to cover speaking only of the worship of one God. Nowhere does it require man to worship the sun, the moon etc. In fact there are clear statements to the contrary:[14]

$$...\text{لَا تَسْجُدُوا لِلشَّمْسِ وَ لَا لِلْقَمَرِ وَاسْجُدُوا لِلّٰهِ الَّذِيْ خَلَقَهُنَّ}...$$

In other words, do not worship the sun, the moon, or any work of creation, but worship only Him, Who has created you. Apart from this, the Holy Qur'an is itself a testimony to God through its old and new signs. It is a mirror which shows God's existence. Why should it be made the target of such ferocious attacks? Why are we not treated in the same spirit as we treat the Āryās? And why is the seed of enmity and hatred sown in the soil of this country? Do they really expect that the outcome of such behaviour will be good? Is it decent to hurl stones at one who offers flowers or to splash urine on one who offers milk?

If Hindus and those belonging to the Āryā faith were prepared to make a complete truce whereby they accept our Prophet, (may peace and blessings of Allah be upon him) to be a true Prophet of God and in future agree to refrain from contempt and slander, then I am ready to be the first to sign the following treaty:

> We, the members of the Ahmadiyyah Jamā'at, will testify to the truth of the origin of the Vedas, and will speak of the Vedas and their Rishis with respect and love, and if we do not honour our part of the contract, we will be liable to pay a fine of not less than three hundred thousand rupees to the Hindu community.

---

14. (*Ḥā Mīm al-Sajdah*, 41:38)

If the Hindus genuinely desire to effect a compromise with us, then they should also write it as a declaration and sign it; its subject matter being as follows:

> We believe in the divine message and Prophethood of Hadrat Muhammad *Mustafā Rasūlullāh* [the chosen one, the Messenger of Allah] may peace and blessings of Allah be upon him, and deem him to be a true Prophet and Messenger. From now on we will remember him with reverence and respect as befits a believer. If this is not adhered to, a large fine of not less than three hundred thousand rupees will be paid to leader of the Ahmadiyyah Jamā'at.

It should be remembered that at present, the Ahmadiyyah Jamā'at numbers not less than four hundred thousand[15]. Hence, the collection of three hundred thousand rupees should not be considered too great a task for such an important cause. The majority of people who are outside the fold of our Jamā'at are disunited in their views and are diverse in their nature. They do not follow a leader, obedience to whom they would consider incumbent. This is why I cannot undertake anything on their behalf; as yet they consider me to be a *kāfir* [imposter] and *dajjāl* [Antichrist]. But I trust that when the Hindus enter into an agreement with me, they[16] will also not be so daring as to abuse the Book and the Rishis of such a civilized people and thereby invite the abuse of the Holy Prophet (may peace and blessings of Allah be upon him) in retaliation. Such abuses will then be rightly blamed on those who act irresponsibly. As such action is contrary to modest

---

15. This number represents the membership as of the writing of this book in 1908. [Publisher]
16. The other Muslims [Publisher]

and virtuous behaviour, I do not expect that after this treaty they would permit their tongues to wag. It should be mandatory that to make the contract binding, ten thousand adult representatives from both parties should sign it.

My dear ones, there is nothing like peace and compromise. Let us unite with the blessing of this treaty and be one nation. You know full well that denial[17] on both sides has thrown us apart and that our country is suffering greatly. Visualise how blessed it could prove to testify to each other's truth. Come, give this a try now. This is the best course for achieving peace. Pursuing any other course would be like ignoring a dangerous abscess merely because it looks clear and shiny, while, in reality, it contains rotten and putrid matter.

I need not elaborate on the ever-increasing, mutually hypocritical, attitude and discord between the Hindus and Muslims. This is rooted not in religious differences alone, but has also secondary causes which pertain to worldly ambitions. For instance, the Hindus have always shown their desire to have more say in the affairs of government and country. They have been demanding that they should, at the very least, always be consulted in such affairs and that the government should always pay special attention to their demands. They also desire that they be posted at the higher ranking offices as the British are. The Muslims made the blunder of not joining this campaign of Hindus out of fear that they were small in numbers. They were afraid that whatever benefit was to be had from such campaigns would be drawn by the majority Hindu community and not the Muslims. So they not only

---

17. i.e. denial of each other's holy personages. [Publisher]

abstained from joining this cause, but they also obstructed the passage of Hindu efforts by openly opposing it. Thus mutual enmity increased.

I admit that such factors contributed to furthering the enmity which had already existed. But I cannot accept them to be the real reason. I beg to differ with those who believe that religious disputes are not at the root of Hindu-Muslim enmity and discord, and that the disputes are in fact political in nature.

Everyone can easily understand why Muslims are reluctant to join forces with Hindus in demanding their due rights and why they have been refusing to join Congress and why again, having perceived the soundness of the Hindu strategy, they began to follow the same path step after step while maintaining a distinct and separate entity, taking great care not to be identified with them. They did not join the Hindus, but created a similar but separate Muslim organisation.[18]

Dear Friends! I reassert that the underlying factor responsible for this behaviour is religion, and nothing else. If today the same Hindus embrace the Muslims while pronouncing the *kalimah Tayyibah*:[19]

$$\text{لَآ اِلٰهَ اِلَّا اللّٰهُ مُحَمَّدٌ رَّسُوْلُ اللّٰهِ}$$

then Muslims would cease to oppose them forthwith. Conversely, if Muslims renounce Islam and embrace Hinduism and start worshipping fire, air, etc., in accordance

---

18. The organisation was called Muslim League and was established in 1906. [Publisher]
19. There is none worthy of worship except Allah; Muḥammad is the messenger of Allah. [Publisher]

with the Vedic injunctions[20], then those differences which are labelled as political will suddenly vanish as if they had never existed.

It is thus evident that the underlying factors in all enmities and grudges are the religious differences. It is such religious differences which, since times immemorial, reach a climax and then invariably give way to extensive bloodshed.

O Muslims, I say: If Hindus treat you as a different nation merely because of religious differences and you respond to them in the same manner, the matter will not end here. How can you achieve a sound, healthy relationship unless you take appropriate remedial measures against this root cause? It is possible that you may temporarily enjoy a friendship, but only superficially. The ultimate sincerity of heart, worthy of being called sincerity, can only be achieved if you genuinely change your attitude towards the Vedas and the Vedic Rishis by accepting them to be from God. Likewise, the Hindus should also change their niggardly attitude by testifying to the truth of our beloved Holy Prophet (may peace and blessings of Allah be upon him). Remember, and remember it well, that this is the only principle which can establish a genuine truce between you and the Hindus and this is the only water which can wash away all malice embittering your relationship. If the hour has finally come when these two nations, who have for so long fallen apart, are destined to be reunited, then God will open up their hearts to this purpose as He has already opened up our hearts to the same.

---

20. The reference is to today's distorted Vedic injunctions that have been modified over time by the followers. [Publisher]

It is essential however that you treat Hindus with sincerity and kindness and let decent behaviour be your second nature. Refrain from all such measures as would cause them pain, except those that are essential or obligatory according to our faith. Consequently if the Hindus sincerely accept the proposition of testifying to the truth of our Holy Prophet (may peace and blessings of Allah be upon him) and of having faith in his truth, then what remains regarding the split on the issue of cows can be done away with. Remember if we are permitted to eat something, it does not follow that we have to eat it. Everything permissible is not obligatory. There are many things which we know to be lawful yet we do not necessarily practice them. To treat Hindus with decency and kindness is one of the important Islamic injunctions—. If for the sake of achieving a higher goal one forgoes a right, it will not be against the spirit of the Divine law. To consider something to be lawful is one thing, to utilise it is another. The spirit of piety requires that you abstain from whatever God has forbidden. To actually pursue the path of gaining His favour and to have the welfare of His creation at heart and to treat others with goodness and sympathy and to respect all the holy Prophets and Messengers from God, and to accept them as reformers and to not discriminate between them and to serve all mankind irrespective of denominations. This is the essential requirement of our faith. How can we ever be at peace with such people who—without justification and without regard for the fear of Allah—speak of our Holy Prophet, Ḥaḍrat Muḥammad (may peace and blessings of Allah be upon him) with disrespect, and abuse him and refrain not from the use of foul language? In truth, I declare that it is possible for us to make peace with the serpents fed on brackish soil and the wolves of the wilderness, but not with those who make wanton attacks on our Holy Prophet (may peace and blessings of Allah be upon him) who is dearer to us than our lives, our mothers and our fathers. May Allah cause us to die as Muslims. We are not willing to do anything at the cost of our faith.

Here, I do not wish to censure any particular people nor do I intend to hurt anyone's feelings. But, with a deep sense of mortification, I observe that Islam, being a religion of peace, never attacked the founder of any religion. The Qur'an is that revered book which laid the foundation of peace between nations and acknowledged the truth of all Prophets belonging to all the different nations. It is the Holy Qur'an which enjoys the unique distinction of teaching us with regards to the Prophets of the entire world that:[21]

... لَا نُفَرِّقُ بَيْنَ اَحَدٍ مِّنْهُمْ وَنَحْنُ لَهُ مُسْلِمُوْنَ ۙ

Therefore, O Muslims, you should declare: We believe in all the Prophets of God belonging to this world and we do not discriminate between them as to reject one and accept the others.

Name one book like the Holy Qur'an which is so dedicated for the cause of peace. The universal beneficence of God has not been confined by the Qur'an to any specific House. It acknowledges the Prophets of the House of Israel, one and all, be they Jacob[as], Isaac[as], Moses[as], David[as] or Jesus[as]. And it acknowledges the Prophets of other nations regardless of whether they dwelt in India or Persia. None of them have

---

21. We make no distinction between any of them, and to Him we submit. (*Āl-e-'Imrān*, 3:85) [Publisher]

been labeled as deceitful or imposters. On the contrary, it clearly proclaims that Prophets appeared in every nation and in every township and laid the foundation of peace between all the peoples. Alas, this Messenger of Peace is abused and treated with contempt by all peoples alike.

O my dear countrymen, I have not expressed this view to offend you or to hurt your sensibilities in any way. But I do desire to submit, in all sincerity, that those who have made it their second nature to vilify the Prophets of other faiths and consider this unjustified behaviour to be a part of their faith commit an act of unwarranted interference in others' affairs. They not only sin against God, but they are also guilty of sowing the seed of discord and enmity among mankind. Now answer me with hand on heart: if someone abuses another's father or accuses another's mother of unchaste conduct, will this not be tantamount to assailing the honour of his father himself? If anyone retaliates with similar abuses, will it not be appropriate to say that in reality the blame lies with the person who initiated it? In that case he himself would be the offender of his parents' honour.

God, through the Holy Qur'an, has cultivated refined and respectful etiquettes. He admonishes:[22]

...لَا تَسُبُّوا الَّذِيْنَ يَدْعُوْنَ مِنْ دُوْنِ اللّٰهِ
فَيَسُبُّوا اللّٰهَ عَدْوًۢا بِغَيْرِ عِلْمٍ...

In other words, do not even abuse the idols of the non-believers lest they abuse your God out of ignorance. (*sūrah al-Anʿām*, al-juzw, 7)

---

22. (*al-Anʿām*, 6:109)

Now consider that this is the Qur'anic teaching despite the fact that it treats idols as of no significance. Yet God teaches the Muslims to abstain from insulting even the idols and admonishes them instead to adopt a course of gentle persuasion lest they [the idolaters] should be provoked, in turn, to abuse God. The Muslims would then be responsible for such abuses. What manner of people are they who revile the name of this great Prophet of Islam and speak of him with utter disrespect, brutally assailing his honour and tarnishing his spotless character. He is the highly revered Prophet whose name is held in such awe as when uttered the great Muslim kings vacate their thrones and bow their heads to his commands. They consider it an honour to be counted among the humblest of his servants. Is this respect not a bounty of God? Those who dare insult the recipient of such honour do, in fact, quarrel with God Himself. The Holy Prophet Muhammad (may peace and blessings of Allah be upon him) holds such a high station with God that to prove his truth He has shown the world great miracles. Is this not the work of His Mighty hand, which has bowed the heads of 200 million people before Muhammad's threshold? Granted that every Prophet had many a heavenly signs in his support, but the peerless signs shown in Muhammad's support outnumber them all. They continue to appear even today as they were manifested in the past.

Alas, you cannot understand an argument as plain as this: When the earth is filled with sin and becomes uncouth and when wickedness, debauchery, and impertinence weigh heavier on the scale of God than acts of righteousness, it is then that God's mercy requires of Him to send one of His servants who would set the disorder right. Sickness and disease call for a healer. You of all people should be able to understand this better than others. You hold the view that the Vedas were not revealed at a time when the ocean of sin was in spate, but that they were revealed, instead when the calm of sinlessness prevailed over land and sea. Do you then consider it inconceivable that a Prophet should appear when the flood of sin rages high and rapidly inundates every country of the world?

I do hope that you are not so ignorant of the facts of history. When our Holy Prophet (may peace and blessings of Allah be upon him) honoured the office of prophethood with his advent, the age had plunged into utter darkness and no aspect of human conduct was free from the blemish of sin and false beliefs. Pundit Dyanand writes in his book *Satyarath Parkash,* that even in the land of Āryāwart [which takes pride in its monotheistic beliefs] idolatry had replaced the worship of God, and the Vedic faith had become extensively corrupted.

Reverend Pfander, a white European priest and a staunch defender of Christian faith, also endorses these views in his book, *Mīzān-ul-Ḥaq*. He observes that at the time of the inception of Islam, the Christians had become the most corrupt among all the religious denominations. The lewd and wanton conduct of the Christians of the time was a source of shame and dishonour for Christianity. The Holy Qur'an, justifying its revelation, speaks of the same in the following verse[23]:

$$\ldots ظَهَرَ الْفَسَادُ فِي الْبَرِّ وَ الْبَحْرِ$$

---

23. (*al-Rūm*, 30:42)

That is: Corruption has appeared on the land and the sea. This verse implies that every nation, whether in a state of ignorance or whether it presumed itself to be wise, was not free from corruption.

Thus it is established on the authority of all testimonies that the entire mankind, during the age of Prophet Muḥammad (may peace and blessings of Allah be upon him) were they oriental or occidental, those belonging to the land of Āryās or those who were dwellers of the Arabian desert, so also those who inhabited islands, had all become moral destitutes. There was not one among them whose relation with God was without blemish. Evil practices contaminated the entire earth. Why then cannot a man of sound mind understand this simple matter of commonsense that it was the right time and the right age, with reference to which human reason can accept, that an exceptionally eminent Prophet must be raised.

As to the question concerning the reformation which this Prophet brought about with his advent, none can answer like a Muslim with reference to the overwhelming evidence of the great reformation brought about by the Holy Prophet of Islam (may peace and blessings of Allah be upon him). It is beyond the scope of a Christian, Jew or Āryan to answer this question with such clarity and with the support of such irrefutable evidence.

The first phase of the Holy Prophet's (may peace and blessings of Allah be upon him) reformation began with that of the Arabs. The Arabian peninsula was in such a hapless state that it was hard to refer to its dwellers as humans. Name an evil which they did not exhibit; name a form of idolatry which they did not practise. To steal and rob was the order of the day, and committing pointless murder was like trampling an insignificant ant under their feet. They murdered innocent children and usurped all that belonged to them. It was not rare for them to bury their daughters alive. They took pride in fornication and boasted of it in their songs. Drinking was so common among them that there was no house without cellars of wine. They led the whole world in gambling. Beasts would feel ashamed at being likened to them and snakes and wolves would be disgraced if called Arabs.

When our Prophet (may peace and blessings of Allah be upon him) stood up with a resolve to reform them and decided to cleanse their hearts with all his spiritual intent, within a matter of a short time they displayed such rapid changes as transformed them from beasts into humans and then from ordinary humans into a cultured people and from a cultured people they became Godly and became totally immersed in the love of God. For the sake of that love they suffered every torture as though their sense of pain had been paralyzed. They were subjected to extreme suffering by different modes of torture and were ruthlessly flogged. They were made to lie on burning sand and imprisoned. They were deprived of food and water until they reached the verge of death; but at every trial they continued to march forward. There were so many among them whose children were slain before their very eyes and there were many among them who were themselves crucified in front of their children.

The singular devotion with which they laid down their lives is such that even to think of it agitates one to tears. If it is not the command of God and the power of spiritual attention of His Prophet, which worked magic on their hearts, what else could it have been which gravitated them so irresistibly towards Islam? What magic transformed them and made them bow on the threshold of a humble man who had once treaded the streets of Mecca without any kind of friendship, wealth, or power? There had to be a spiritual hand which lifted them from such lowly depths to such dazzling heights. Even more amazing is the fact that many among them were those who, in their earlier stages of rejection, were sworn enemies of the Holy Prophet (may peace and blessings of Allah be upon him) and thirsty after his blood. I see no greater miracle than this that one so helpless, poor and penniless as he, could wash their hearts of all the stains of enmity and hatred and draw them so powerfully towards himself. So much so that they cast away their royal garments willingly for the sake of God and accepted the humility of being clothed in sackcloth.

Some, in their ignorance, blame Islam of *Jihad* [waging wars] to spread its message and of gaining converts at the point of sword. They claim that these converts were forced to change their religion under the threat of the sword. Woe to them a thousand times! They have exceeded all limits in their injustice and in their efforts to conceal the truth. O pity! What is wrong with them, that they wilfully turn away from realities? Our Holy Prophet (may peace and blessings of Allah be upon him) did not appear in the land of Arabia in the capacity of a monarch. It therefore cannot be suspected that he had royal majesty and power with him, such that the people gathered under his banner for fear of their lives.

Now the question one faces is simply this: When he waged his lone spiritual battle for the pronouncement of

God's Unity and for the establishment of the truth of his ministry in a state of utter helplessness and poverty, then where was that sword which struck terror in their hearts, and coerced the meek into submission? And had they refused to believe or had they persisted in their rejection of him, from which king did he beg for a contingent army to be sent to his aid so that they may be forced to yield?

O seekers of truth! Rest assured that all these allegations are fabrications by those who are sworn enemies of Islam. Cast a glance at history. Muḥammad (may peace and blessings of Allah be upon him) was that same orphan whose father died shortly after his birth and whose mother passed away leaving him behind as a child of only a few months. That child on whom God had extended His hand of support was nurtured in His care without any other patronage. During those hard times of orphanhood, he tended goats belonging to others. None was his mentor except God. And even up to the age of twenty-five, none of his uncles were willing to offer their daughter's hand in marriage to him as it appeared that he would be unable to meet even the basic household expenses. Moreover, he was unlettered and was not trained in any skill or profession. As he approached the age of forty, lo, there he was with his heart powerfully drawn towards his Lord, Allah, the Gracious. There was a cave, a few miles from Mecca by the name of Ḥira. It was here that he would retire by himself and, concealed from the eyes of men, become lost in the remembrance of God. One day, in that very cave, while he was praying in seclusion, God revealed Himself to him, and he was told: The people have turned their backs on the path of Allah and the earth is befouled with sin. So I [God

Almighty] appoint you as My Messenger and send you to the world, so that you may warn the people that they should turn back to their Lord before His punishment befalls them.

Being unlettered, he was frightened by this command and beseeched God: I know not how to read and write. Then God filled his bosom with all faculties of spiritual knowledge and enlightened his heart. With the blessing of his *quwwat-e-qudsiyyah* [power of purification], the humble and meek started entering the circle of obedience to him. But the powerful leaders mustered all their forces to oppose him tooth and nail. They went even to the length of plotting to kill him and many men and many women were put to agonising death. As a last measure they surrounded the house of the Holy Prophet (may peace and blessings of Allah be upon him) with intent to murder him. But who can touch him whom God protects. God revealed to him: Leave this town forthwith and I will remain with you at every step.

Accordingly he left Mecca and took Abū Bakr (may Allah be pleased with him) along and remained in hiding for three nights in the cave of Thaur. The enemy gave chase, and with the aid of a tracker were led to the cave. That tracker traced their footsteps right up to the entrance of the cave, telling them: Here the track ends, so search for him in this cave. If he is not to be found here then the sky must have swallowed him. Who can limit the boundless wonders of God's creation? In a single night, God so manifested His will that a spider spun its web across the mouth of the cave from end to end and a pigeon built its nest at the entrance of the cave and even laid its eggs therein. When the tracker urged the Meccans to enter the cave, an old man thus retorted: This tracker must be mad. I have been seeing this web across the mouth of the cave since the time when Muḥammad (may peace and blessings of Allah be upon him) was not even born. At this, people began to disperse and gave up the idea of searching the cave.

After this, the Holy Prophet (may peace and blessings of Allah be upon him) travelled to Medina secretly. The majority of the inhabitants of Medina accepted him, causing the people of Mecca to seeth in rage, lamenting: Our prey has slipped out of our hands. They then became occupied in plots to murder the Holy Prophet (may peace and blessings of Allah be upon him). A small party from among the Meccans who had accepted Muḥammad (may peace and blessings of Allah be upon him) also left Mecca and migrated to different countries. Some took shelter under the Emperor of Abyssinia[24]. Some however were left behind in Mecca as they lacked adequate provisions for such journeys; they were tormented to the extreme. The Holy Qur'an mentions how they wailed and bemoaned day and night to God.

The cruelties of the infidels from among the Qureish exceeded all bounds. They started to murder the helpless, poor women and orphaned children. They went to the extent of killing some women with such ruthlessness as to have tightly bound their legs each to different camels and driving them in opposite directions. Thus they died as they split in two.

When the transgression of these merciless infidels reached this stage, God, who turns to His servants with mercy revealed to his Messenger: The supplications of the afflicted

---

24. Current day Ethiopia [Publisher]

have reached me. Thus this day, I permit them to stand up to their persecutors and remember that a people who raise their sword against the innocent will themselves perish by the sword. Yet, transgress not, because God does not befriend those who transgress.

This is the spirit and essence of Islamic Jihad which has been maliciously portrayed in the wrong light. God is forbearing, indeed, but when the mischief of a people crosses all limits, then He does not let the transgressors go unpunished. Then He Himself creates conditions which result in their destruction. I know not how and from where our opponents heard that Islam was spread by the might of the sword. God in the Holy Qur'an pronounced that there is no compulsion in Islam:[25]

... لَا إِكْرَاهَ فِى الدِّيْنِ

That is: The religion of Islam does not permit any compulsion in matters of faith. Who commanded the application of force and what were the means of coercion available to them? And again, such people as are coerced into changing their faith do not display such dedication and such quality of belief, that without any financial returns and despite being a mere few hundred they dare to confront the army of thousands. When the same reached the number of one thousand, they somehow acquired the strength to defeat enemies running into hundreds of thousands. They readily offered their lives in defence of their faith, to be slaughtered like sheep and goats. They stamped the testimony to the truth of Islam with their own blood. Moreover, they became so enamoured with the

---

25. (al-Baqarah, 2:257)

task of spreading the Unity of God that, willingly accepting all kinds of hardships like ascetics, they crossed the deserts of Africa to disseminate the message of Islam so that their blessed teachings should bear the fruit of truth. Thus they succeeded in converting tens of millions of Chinese people to Islam. Then they entered India in the style of dervishes wearing sackcloth and succeeded in converting many to Islam from the Āryā faith. They even reached the frontiers of Europe and raised loud and clear the message:[26]

لَآ اِلٰهَ اِلَّا اللّٰهُ

Can you claim in honesty that such as these are really the fruits of the sword of Islam, whose hearts remain infidel while the tongues alone profess the faith. Nay! It is the work of those whose hearts were filled with the light of faith. Nothing but God dwelled in their hearts.

Now we turn our attention to the study of Islamic teachings and its true nature. It should be clearly borne in mind that the predominant purpose of Islamic teachings is to establish the Unity and Majesty of God on earth, to completely eradicate idolatry and to gather all scattered religious denominations around a single article of faith and turn them into one people.

The religions which appeared before Islam and the Prophets and Messengers that came were confined to the reformation of their own respective nation and country; whatever they did for their moral uplift was all aimed for the benefit of their own people. This is why Jesus[as] unambiguously admitted that his teachings were for the House of Israel alone. It is reported that when a woman who did not belong

---

26. There is none worthy of worship except Allah. [Publisher]

to Israelites beseeched him with humility for him to show her 'the way', he rejected her plea. The poor woman even went to the extent of likening herself to a dog to evoke pity, and implored guidance. He again rejected her plea on the ground that he was sent only for the sheep of the House of Israel. Finally, she was silenced. But Our Prophet (may peace and blessings of Allah be upon him) nowhere pronounced that he had been sent only for the Arabs. On the contrary, the Holy Qur'an commands him to say:[27]

$$\text{... قُلْ يَٰٓأَيُّهَا ٱلنَّاسُ إِنِّى رَسُولُ ٱللَّهِ إِلَيْكُمْ جَمِيعًا}$$

That is, tell the people that I am a Messenger to you all from Allah. It should be remembered that it was no fault of Jesus[as] that he gave such a curt answer to the woman. The time had not yet come for a universal teaching. This was the teaching vouchsafed to Jesus[as] by God: You are specifically sent for the House of Israel. You have no concern with others.

As I mentioned above, the moral teachings of Jesus were confined to the Jews. The Torah taught "a tooth for a tooth, an eye for an eye, and an ear for the ear"[28]. The purport of the teaching was to provide a commandment to the Jews to establish justice and prevent them from committing transgressions and excesses. This was necessary because having spent four hundred years in slavery, cruelty and meanness had become their second nature. Hence the profound Wisdom of God so planned that to counter the overemphasis of cruelty and revenge in their natures, the teachings of forgiveness and

---

27. (*al-A'rāf*, 7:159)
28. See (*Exodus*, 21:24), (*Leviticus*, 24:20), and (*Deuteronomy*, 19:21). [Publisher]

love was highly stressed to the same degree. Hence the moral teaching found in the Gospels is specifically for the Jews and not for the whole world as Jesus[as] had no concern with other people.

The teaching which Jesus[as] brought did not only have the drawback of not being addressed to all mankind, but it also had another shortcoming. As Torah overemphasises revenge to one extreme, the Gospels, turn to the other extreme as regards the teaching of forgiveness. Both these scriptures fail to bring into focus all the possible branches of human nature. As for Torah, it remains concerned with only one branch, while the Gospels hold fast to the other exclusively. Both teachings lack balance. As it is evident that to punish on every occasion is not appropriate nor is it in accordance with the dictates of justice, likewise to forgive and to overlook faults indiscriminately is contrary to the spirit of human reform. In view of this the Holy Qur'an does not entirely agree with either, but instead proposes the following:[29]

وَجَزَٰٓؤُا۟ سَيِّئَةٍ سَيِّئَةٌ مِّثْلُهَا ۖ فَمَنْ عَفَا وَأَصْلَحَ فَأَجْرُهُ عَلَى ٱللَّهِ...

So an injury can only be avenged to the extent of the injury received, as is taught by the Torah. But whoever prefers to forgive, as is taught by the Gospels, then such forgiveness is only permitted when the person forgiven is likely to respond with reform and the final outcome is positive and healthy and the whole episode ends up well. Otherwise, the routine teaching remains the same as that of the Torah.

---

29. The recompense of an injury is an injury the like thereof; but whoso forgives and his act brings about reformation, his reward is with Allah. (*al-Shūrā*, 42:41) [Publisher]

GLOSSARY

Abū Bakr—A close friend and companion of the Holy Prophet[sa] and the first caliph in Islam. He was the first among men to confirm the truth of the claim of the Holy Prophet[sa].

Allah—Allah is the personal name of God in Islam. To show proper reverence to Him, Muslims often add *Taʿālā,* 'the Most High', when saying His Holy name.

Aḥmadī Muslim or Aḥmadī—A member of the Aḥmadiyyah Muslim Jamāʿat.

Aḥmadiyyah Muslim Jamāʿat—The Community of Muslims who accept the claims of Hadrat Mirzā Ghulām Ahmad[as] of Qadian as being the Promised Messiah and Mahdī; the Jamāʿat was established by Hadrat Mirzā Ghulām Ahmad[as] in 1889, and is now under the leadership of his fifth Khalīfah, Hadrat Mirzā Masroor Ahmad[aba].

Al-Imām al-Mahdī—The title given to the Promised Reformer of the latter days; it means guided leader.

Āryā or Āryā Samāj—A movement founded in 1875 by Swāmī Dayānanda in India with the objective of promoting the teachings of the Vedas.

Āryan—A member of the Āryā group.

Āryawart—Land of the Āryās—India.

Bābā Nānak—Believed by the Sikhs to be the founder of their religion, Bābā Nānak (1469-1539) was actually a Muslim. He performed Ḥajj, married into a Muslim family, and lived a pious life.

Ganges—A river in the northern part of India revered by Hindus and believed to facilitate salvation for those who bathe in it.

Ḥaḍrat—A term of respect used for a person of established righteousness and piety.

Ḥajj—Pilgrimage to the House of Allah in Mecca, Arabia; also known as the fifth pillar of Islam.

Holy Prophet[sa]—A term used exclusively for Ḥaḍrat Muḥammad[sa], the Prophet of Islam.

Holy Qur'an—The Book sent by Allah for the guidance of mankind. It was revealed to the Holy Prophet Muhammad[sa] over a period of twenty-three years.

Jainism—A religion and philosophy originating in India around 500 BC by Prince Vardhamāna (known by his followers as Mahavira) who was born into a Hindu family but later took exception to some of the common teachings of the Hindu religion, including the caste system.

Jamāʻat—Jamāʻat means community. Although the word Jamāʻat itself may refer to any community, in this book, Jamāʻat specifically refers to the Aḥmadiyyah Muslim Jamāʻat.

Jihad—The literal translation of this word is 'striving'. The term is used to mean self-purification as well as religious wars in some instances.

Kalimah—The declaration of the Islamic faith: 'There is none worthy of worship except Allah; Muhammad[sa] is the Messenger of Allah.' It is also known as the first pillar of Islam.

Mahdī—*See* al-Imām al-Mahdī.

Nyog—A practice allowing a woman who has not been able to get an issue from her husband to co-habit with some other person and produce children for her husband.

(The) Promised Messiah—This term refers to the Founder of the Aḥmadiyyah Muslim Jamā'at, Ḥaḍrat Mirzā Ghulām Aḥmad[as] of Qadian. He claimed that he had been sent by Allah in accordance with the prophecies of the Holy Prophet Muḥammad[sa] concerning the coming of *al-Imām al-Mahdī* and Messiah from among the Muslims.

Pundit—A term used to denote respect or status in the Hindu religion. Pundits are traditionally known to have memorized a substantial portion of the Vedas and conduct religious services for Hindus.

Rishīs—A Hindu term for religious divines who sever all ties with the material world and submit completely to acts of devotion.

Ṣāḥib—A term of respect for a man, similar to the diversity of English terms like mister or sir.

Samāj—A Hindu term for society.

Shakat Faith—A sect in Hinduism.

Srī Krishnā—A prophet of God in Hinduism known to have been born around 1458 BC.

Sūrah—A term in Arabic referring to a chapter of the Holy Qur'an.

Vedas—Religious texts of Hinduism.

Zend-Avesta—means commentaries on Avesta, the sacred texts of the Zoroastrian religion. In the context of this book, it refers to the Zoroastrian religion.

Zoroastrians—Followers of a religion based on the teachings of Prophet Zoroaster[as].

SUBJECT INDEX

A

Allah the Almighty
  all religions originated from, 23
  attributes of, teach kindness and magnanimity 6
  belief in, unites humanity 5, 7, 42
  communion with, 8, 13, 15, 38
  divine decree, 15
  humanity needs to cultivate attributes of, 6, 10
  Jewish beliefs about, 17
  treats all people equally, 6, 10, 16
  universal concept in Islam, 7, 10, 43
  universal concept missing in other religions 7, 16, 20, 42

B

Bābā Nānak
  ignored by Hindus, 15
  mission of, 15
  relics of, printed with Islamic teachings 14
  testifies to Islam's truth 14
Buddha, Gautum
  branded as an atheist 19
  mission of, 19

C

Christianity
  beliefs about communion with Allah the Almighty 8
  beliefs about Prophets and Messengers 7

H

Hindus of India
  beliefs about communion with Allah the Almighty among Āryāh sect 8
  common ground with Jews and Christians 8
  proposal of truce for, 12, 25
  religious differences at root of hostility with Muslims of India 28
  unity needed with Muslims of India 5, 11, 27
Holy Prophet Muhammad[sa]
  difficult life of, 38
  high status of, 33
  reformation brought by, 35
  time for sending, 34
Humanity
  equal treatment from Allah the Almighty to all, 6
  need to cultivate attributes of Allah the Almighty 6, 10, 12

united through belief in Allah the Almighty 5, 7, 42
unity acquired through respect and mutual sympathy 6, 11, 12, 22, 25, 27, 29, 30, 32

I

Islam
abuse and horrific torture of followers of, 36, 40
beliefs about Prophets and Messengers 9
common ground with Vedic teachings 13
compulsion not acceptable in, 41
effects of the message 36
misconceptions about, 37, 41
permission granted to fight for oppressed 40
respect for all Prophets and Messengers, 22, 25, 31
teaches peace among religions 32
universal concept of Allah the Almighty 7, 9, 22, 43

J

Jesus[as]
critique of the godhead attributed to, 8
mission of, 42
Judaism
beliefs about Allah Almighty, 17
beliefs about Prophets and Messengers 7

M

Muslims of India
proposal of truce for, 12, 25
religious differences root of hostility with Hindus of India 28
unity needed with Hindus of India 5, 11, 27

P

Promised Messiah[as]
prayer for guidance by, 5
truce proposed to India's Muslims and Hindus 12, 25
warning to nations 6
Prophets and Messengers
appeared worldwide 9, 16
criterion for true, 23
Gautum Buddha 19
Islam respects all, 22, 25, 31
Islamic beliefs about, 9
Jewish and Christian beliefs about, 7
Srī Krishnā 13

R

Religion(s)
beliefs about communion with Allah the Almighty 8
compulsion not acceptable in Islam 41
criterion for true, 6
Islam teaches peace among, 32
originated from Allah the Almighty 23
unaware of other existing, 20
universal concept of Allah the Almighty missing in, other than Islam 7, 16, 20, 42

S

Sympathy
humanity needs to cultivate, 6
required in religion 6